ALL ABOUT
NEW ZEALAND
BIRDS

Dave Gunson

NEW
HOLLAND

Also from Dave Gunson and New Holland Publishers:

ISBN 978-1-86966-290-5

ISBN 978-1-86966-296-7

ISBN 978-1-86966-217-2

ISBN 978-1-86966-251-6

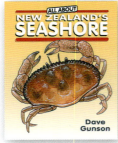

ISBN 978-1-86966-252-3

ISBN 978-1-86966-284-4

ISBN 978-1-86966-282-0

ISBN 978-1-86966-297-4

978-1-86966-235-6

978-1-86966-405-3

978-1-86966-384-1

978-1-86966-334-6

978-1-86966-285-1

978-1-86966-389-6

First published in 2008 by New Holland Publishers (NZ) Ltd
Auckland • Sydney • London • Cape Town

www.newhollandpublishers.co.nz

218 Lake Road, Northcote, Auckland 0627, New Zealand
Unit 1, 66 Gibbes Street, Chatswood, NSW 2067, Australia
The Chandlery, Unit 114, 50 Westminster Bridge Road, London,
   SE1 7QY, United Kingdom
Wembley Square, First Floor, Solan Road, Gardens, Cape Town 8001,
   South Africa

Publishing manager: Christine Thomson
Commissioned by Louise Armstrong
Editor: Katrina Rainey
Design: Janine Brougham and Dave Gunson

10 9 8 7 6 5 4 3

Colour reproduction by SC (Sang Choy) International Pte Ltd, Singapore
Printed in China by Toppan Leefung Printing Ltd, on paper sourced
from sustainable forests.

National Library of New Zealand Cataloguing-in-Publication Data

Gunson, Dave.
All about New Zealand birds / Dave Gunson.
 Includes index.
ISBN 978-1-86966-198-4
1. Birds—New Zealand—Juvenile literature. 2. Birds—
Identification—Juvenile literature. [1. Birds—New Zealand.
2. Birds.] I. Gunson, Dave. II. Title.
 398.0993—dc 22

Contents

Introduction

Probably the first animal that you'll notice when you walk out of your front door is a bird. And the first thing you'll notice about that bird is likely to be its head and bill, which will usually give you some idea of what type of bird it is, and how it lives. Many birds have what might be called 'ordinary' bills, such as those of the blackbird or the song thrush. There's nothing very unusual about the food that they like to eat – insects, worms and so on – but birds that prefer to eat something slightly different often have more specialised bills.

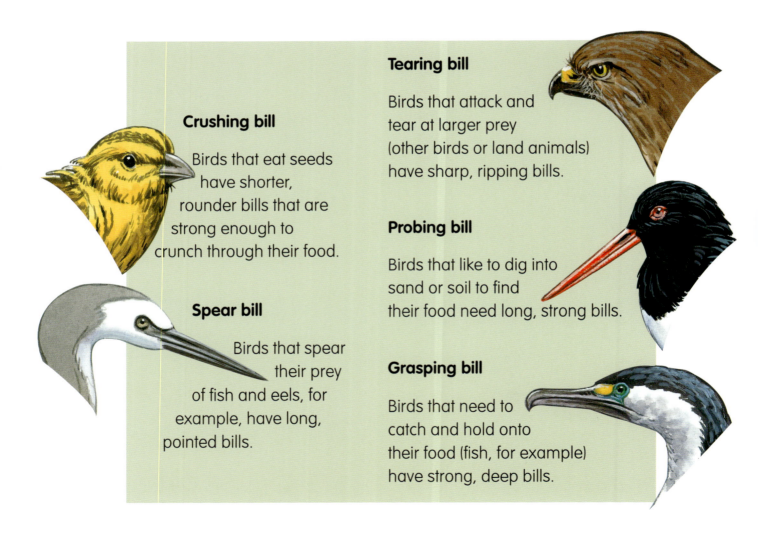

Crushing bill

Birds that eat seeds have shorter, rounder bills that are strong enough to crunch through their food.

Spear bill

Birds that spear their prey of fish and eels, for example, have long, pointed bills.

Tearing bill

Birds that attack and tear at larger prey (other birds or land animals) have sharp, ripping bills.

Probing bill

Birds that like to dig into sand or soil to find their food need long, strong bills.

Grasping bill

Birds that need to catch and hold onto their food (fish, for example) have strong, deep bills.

There are many others types and styles of bill – look at the pictures in this book and see what they can tell you about the way each bird lives and feeds.

About this book

When choosing the birds to show in this book, I tried to find a selection of the interesting birds that can be found in each different environment. Birds are very mobile creatures, though, and you are likely to see many of these birds in more than one of the habitats that I've selected. For example, you might spend all day at the beach and not see a single black-backed gull, and then arrive home to find a pair of them on your house roof, squabbling over a piece of meat that one of them has pinched from the local butcher's shop!

In the pages after the **_Birds of the Past_** section, you'll see a panel for each bird giving the following information:

Weight. This shows the weight of the bird in grams. To give you an idea of weight comparison, an average tomato or kiwifruit weighs about 75–100 grams.

Length. This is the length, in centimetres, of the bird from the tip of its bill to the end of its tail. This book is 26.5 centimetres high and 21 centimetres wide.

Lifespan. This is the number of years that the bird might be expected to live.

Diet. This lists the main items of food that the bird prefers to eat. If it's a small bird, and likes to eat insects, then those insects are probably quite small too – like flies and small beetles. If the bird is large, it might prefer to eat larger insects such as weta and stick insects.

Distribution. This shows the places that you are most likely to see the bird.

Birds of the Past

New Zealand has had many different types of birds, and quite a few of them have been giants or record-breakers of one kind or another.

The fossil remains of at least 13 extinct species of penguin have been found here, including the largest ever known – the New Zealand giant penguin. This bird stood 1.5 metres tall (as tall as an adult human) and probably weighed around 100 kilograms. By comparison, today's emperor penguin stands about 1 metre tall and weighs around 30 kilograms.

Other extinct birds from New Zealand include various ancient species of raven, duck, wren, harrier and a large owl called the laughing owl. The laughing owl got its name from its strong and unusual call, which was a loud cry, followed by a shrieking laugh. It was twice the size of today's morepork, on which it sometimes preyed, but being a ground-dweller, it quickly became a victim of introduced predators because its eggs and chicks were easy prey for rats and dogs. The laughing owl became extinct in the early 1900s.

Miocene False-toothed Pelican

This bird lived around New Zealand coasts about 5–15 million years ago. It was a very large and powerful bird, with a wingspan of about 5.5 metres. The term Miocene refers to the geological era which began about 23 million years ago, and it's not very difficult to see how this bird got the rest of its name – its bill had a series of sharp, jagged points that resembled teeth, and which probably made it a very efficient hunter of fish and squid.

Moa

This is one of the best known of all extinct birds. There were many different species of moa – ranging from some that were the size of a modern-day turkey to giants whose height at the shoulder was as tall as a man. They lived all over New Zealand, in many different habitats – some species lived by the coasts, some in forests and scrub, and some even lived high in the cold mountains.

All other flightless birds show some evidence of their lost ability to fly – tiny wings under their feathers, or

some proof in the shape of their skeleton – but moa show no trace whatsoever of ever having any history of flight.

Forest clearances, hunting and new predators all led to the extinction of moa just before the arrival of European settlers.

Haast's Eagle

Haast's eagle was certainly a giant, which is why it is also known as the New Zealand giant eagle. It was the largest bird of prey that the world has ever seen, with a wingspan of over 3 metres and talons the size of a tiger's! Haast's eagle was large enough to prey on moa and other large flightless birds. It probably kept watch from a high perch for suitable prey crossing open ground, and would then swoop down at speeds over 80 kilometres an hour to make the kill.

After the arrival of human settlers, the numbers of large, flightless birds declined and the eagle lost much of its prey. It probably died out several hundred years ago.

Huia

The huia was one of the very few birds in the world where the male and the female have different physical forms; the female's bill was over twice the length of the male's. Both used their bills to dig in rotten bark to get at grubs and insects underneath – though of course the female could do a lot more digging and probing than the male could.

The huia's white-tipped black tail feathers were highly prized by both Maori and Europeans for decoration, and a combination of hunting and introduced predators meant that the huia had died out by 1907.

Grey Warbler

The grey warbler is a native bird and is common throughout the country, though you are more likely to hear its pretty, trailing song than to see it, as this little bird prefers to stay in the protection of foliage and shade, and is very reluctant to come out into the open.

Weight: 6.5 g	
Length: 11 cm	
Lifespan: 10 years	
Diet: Insects and spiders	
Distribution: Nationwide	

The grey warbler builds a hanging, pear-shaped nest with a very small side entrance – all of which gives it good protection against rats, though not against the shining cuckoo which sometimes lays its eggs in the warbler's nests.

The grey warbler eats mostly insects and spiders, and will even 'hover' for a few seconds to snatch prey from hard-to-reach leaves and branches.

Also known as the waxeye or white-eye, the silvereye was first seen in New Zealand in 1832, and then again in 1835 when a number of birds arrived from Australia at Milford Sound. Larger flocks then arrived in Waikanae, near Wellington, in 1856, and since then the silvereye has spread throughout the country.

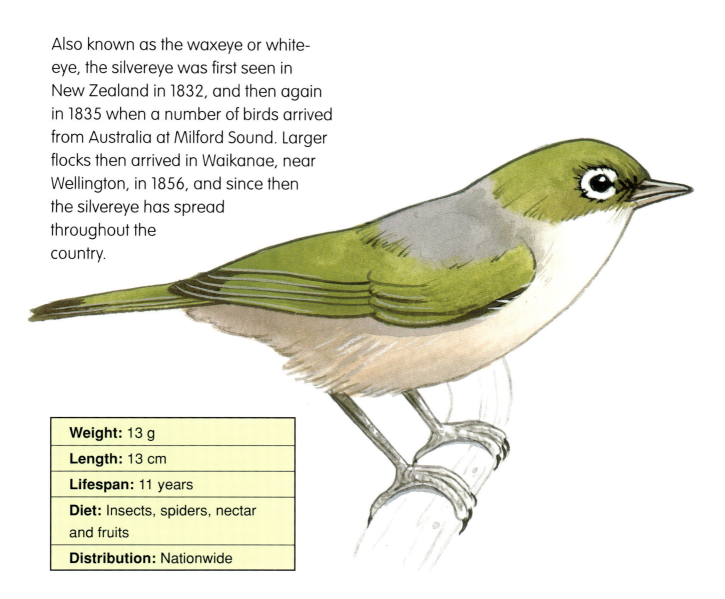

Weight: 13 g	
Length: 13 cm	
Lifespan: 11 years	
Diet: Insects, spiders, nectar and fruits	
Distribution: Nationwide	

Like the tui and the bellbird, the silvereye has a brush-like tongue, which helps it take nectar from flowers. It will quickly appear in suburban gardens if bread, fruit or sugar-water is left out on a bird table. Silvereyes always seem to be much quicker than house sparrows to take whatever scraps are left outside.

Weight:	22 g
Length:	15 cm
Lifespan:	10 years
Diet:	Insects, spiders, seeds and fruits
Distribution:	Nationwide

Introduced into New Zealand by settlers in the 1860s, the chaffinch has now spread to all parts of the country – from parks and gardens, to farmland, forests and even high into the mountains. This hardy little bird has even found its way to some of the subantarctic islands, including Campbell Island. It's become by far the most common of all the finch-like birds that have been introduced into New Zealand – such as the greenfinch, redpoll, goldfinch, yellowhammer and the cirl bunting.

The chaffinch has also been known as the 'bachelor bird' because hundreds of birds of the same sex sometimes flock together.

Its call is a simple *pink pink* but its full song ends in a flourish that has been written down as *chip chip chip tell tell tell cherry-erry-erry tissi cheweeo*.

Yellowhammer

The yellowhammer was introduced into New Zealand in the 1860s, and quickly became a nuisance to farmers and gardeners because it likes to eat seeds. For this reason many birds were killed as pests.

Yellowhammers can be seen in all kinds of country, from alpine tussock to the exposed seashore. They will visit gardens and parks, though they are most common in open country and farmland.

The yellowhammer's song of *tintintintintink-swee* has sometimes been written down as 'a little bit of bread and no cheese'.

Weight: 27 g	
Length: 16 cm	
Lifespan: 10 years	
Diet: Seeds, spiders, insects and grubs	
Distribution: Nationwide	

13

The house sparrow was first introduced into New Zealand in the 1860s, and is now our most common city bird. It can be seen in parks, gardens and farmlands throughout most of the country.

House sparrows like to build nests in thick trees, or in and around houses – in gutters, under eaves and even in chimneys.

Sparrows are great scavengers and are always on the lookout for easy pickings and scraps around cafes and supermarkets.

The male bird can be easily identified by the black 'bib' on its front and its stronger colouring, while the female has duller shades of brown and grey.

Weight: 30 g	
Length: 14 cm	
Lifespan: 10–15 years	
Diet: Seeds, cereal crops (e.g. wheat, barley), insects, small fruits, and whatever might be left of your sandwich or piece of cake at the little cafe up the road.	
Distribution: Nationwide, apart from Fiordland and the lower West Coast	

Song Thrush

Song thrushes and blackbirds were brought to New Zealand in the 1860s.

   Just like its close relative the blackbird, the song thrush can often be seen feeding on the ground – hopping or running along to search out insects. The thrush will often stop and cock its head as though listening for movement, but in fact it's just having a better look at the ground. The song thrush also likes to eat snails, and will carry the shell and break it open against a handy stone to expose the snail inside.

   The song of the male song thrush sounds like he's singing: '*Did* you do it? *Did* you do it? *I* saw you! *I* saw you!'

Weight: 70 g	
Length: 23 cm	
Lifespan: 10 years	
Diet: Insects, spiders, fruits, snails and earthworms	
Distribution: Nationwide	

Starling

Weight: 85 g	
Length: 21 cm	
Lifespan: 20 years	
Diet: Snails, spiders, insects, grubs and fruits	
Distribution: Nationwide	

Along with the song thrush and the blackbird, the starling has become one of our most common birds. It's reckoned that the starling might even be the most common bird in the world, with a global population of well over a billion! It has been estimated that some flocks seen in New Zealand have contained over a million birds!

Starlings like to nest in available holes in trees and cliffs, and in man-made structures such as chimneys and ventilation shafts.

When feeding on the ground, the starling will dig into the soil with its bill to search out grubs and worms. It can also snatch up insects while in flight.

Blackbird

The blackbird is probably our most common bird of all, and can be seen in gardens and parks around the country. The male bird is black with a yellow bill, and the female is dull brown with a light brown bill. The young blackbird has dark speckles on its pale chest, and can sometimes be confused with the song thrush.

The blackbird likes to feed on the ground – scratching or flicking at leaves and grass as it searches for insects. Its song is soft and tuneful, but its alarm call is a very distinctive *tchock, tchock*. You can sometimes see the blackbird 'sunbathing' by resting on the ground with wings outspread.

Weight: 90 g	
Length: 25 cm	
Lifespan: 20 years	
Diet: Fruit, seeds, insects, skinks and earthworms	
Distribution: Nationwide	

17

The eastern rosella became established in New Zealand after some caged birds escaped into Auckland's Waitakere Ranges in 1910.

Rosellas live in small groups, and usually nest in holes in forest trees and in the trunks of tree ferns. Though they occasionally eat insects, they mostly prefer plant food – even enjoying the seeds of the scotch thistle.

The rosella's call is a loud *twink twink,* and you might hear several birds calling as they chase one another through the bush in a flash of bright colour.

Weight: 110 g	
Length: 33 cm	
Lifespan: 10 years	
Diet: Seeds, fruits, flowers, shoots and insects	
Distribution: Auckland and Northland, with some small populations around Coromandel, the Wairarapa, Wellington, Canterbury and Otago	

Myna

Weight: 125 g	
Length: 24 cm	
Lifespan: 12 years	
Diet: Grubs, insects, earthworms and fruits	
Distribution: Common in the North Island, north of the Wanganui region	

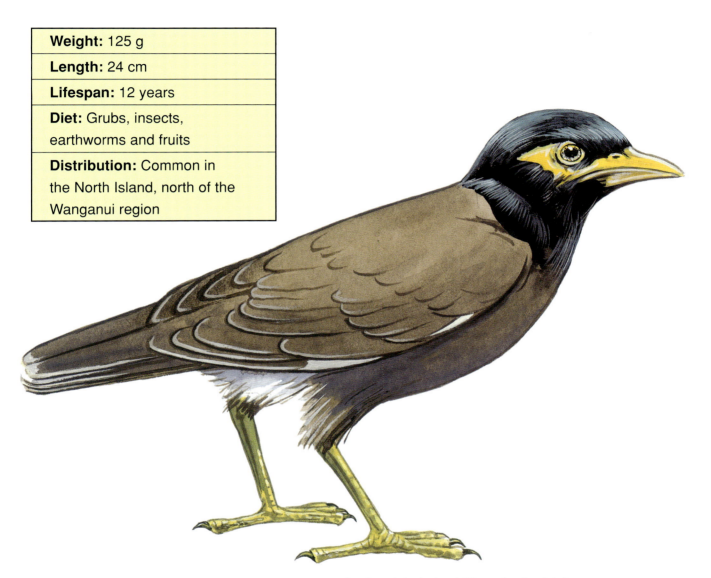

The myna was introduced into New Zealand from India in the 1870s, and has now spread throughout the country.

The myna is a very bold and cheeky bird, and can be seen strutting back and forth across sealed roads, just inches from passing traffic, as it searches for food. Mynas are also very aggressive, and will sometimes take over the nests of other birds by killing their chicks or destroying the eggs.

The myna is a good imitator of sounds, and can copy lots of other birds' songs, as well as the sounds of doorbells and mobile phones. In some countries, mynas are kept as pets and taught to speak human phrases, just like a parrot.

19

The magpie was introduced from Australia in the 1860s to help control insect pests on farms, but was soon found to be very aggressive when protecting its nesting territory. It will attack other birds such as the New Zealand falcon and even the Australasian harrier, which is twice its size.

Weight:	350 g
Length:	41 cm
Lifespan:	20 years
Diet: Seeds, insects, spiders, snails, lizards and carrion (dead animals)	
Distribution: Widespread, except for the West Coast of the South Island	

People passing too close to the bird's nest may find themselves 'dive-bombed' and the bird will sometimes strike at the trespasser's head with open claws.

Magpie nests can be strange affairs; in addition to the usual plant material, magpies will sometimes add lengths of string, pieces of china, cardboard, cloth, glass and even barbed wire!

Rock Pigeon

Weight:	400 g
Length:	33 cm
Lifespan:	3–5 years
Diet:	Seeds, grains, fruits and insects
Distribution:	Nationwide, except for much of the South Island's West Coast and Fiordland

The rock pigeon was introduced into New Zealand by early European settlers, and like its ancestors is very much a bird of towns and cities. They can also be found throughout much of New Zealand's countryside, where they can be a problem for farmers by feeding on new crops of barley, beans, peas and cereals.

In town, the pigeon will nest on any available ledge on buildings; in the country it will nest on rocky outcrops and in caves and depressions in cliffs and banks. Their nests can be an odd assortment of materials, and sometimes include nails and pieces of old metal – one nest found in Wellington was made almost entirely of bits of old wire!

actual size

Weight: 6–7 g (less than the weight of a $1 coin!)
Length: 8 cm
Lifespan: 6 years
Diet: Insects and spiders
Distribution: Found in native and exotic (e.g. pine) forests throughout New Zealand

The rifleman gets its name from the male's green plumage (feathers), which reminded early European settlers of the army's green-jacketed rifle regiments. The Maori name of titipounamu also refers to the bird's green colouring – just like pounamu (greenstone). The female rifleman is similar, but her colours are more olive and grey-brown. And no, she shouldn't be called a rifle*woman*!

The rifleman is a type of wren, and is New Zealand's smallest bird – the illustration shows the bird's actual size.

To feed, the rifleman hops and climbs up tree trunks in a spiral to pick off any insects, grubs or insects it can find there.

Fantail

The friendly little fantail is one of the most common of our native birds, and is often seen and heard around gardens and bush walks as it follows people to snatch up any insects that they might disturb. The fantail hardly ever feeds on the ground, but instead will catch insects in flight, or hover for a few seconds to pick them off leaves and branches. Some will even enter houses during the summer to look for flies, and then take a quick bath under the garden sprinkler.

Many all-black fantails can be seen in the South Island, and sometimes around the Wellington region.

Weight: 8 g	
Length: 16 cm	
Lifespan: 3–10 years	
Diet: Flies, moths, beetles, spiders and fruits	
Distribution: Nationwide	

Weight:	11 g
Length:	13 cm
Lifespan:	10 years
Diet:	Insects, spiders and worms
Distribution:	Forest and scrub areas throughout New Zealand

The tomtit likes to use a low perch in the forest to watch for insects and worms on the forest floor, and then dive down to snatch up its prey. Like other small forest birds, they will often follow bush walkers to see what they might disturb, and sometimes even land on their heads and shoulders to get a better vantage point. Some tomtits have been seen to wash their catch in a nearby creek before offering it to their chicks.

The tomtit's usual call is a simple *swee* or *seet*, but the male can declare his territory with a loud *ti oly oly oly oh*.

Shining Cuckoo

Weight: 25 g
Length: 16 cm
Lifespan: 5–7 years
Diet: Insects
Distribution: Nationwide

Like most other cuckoos around the world, the shining cuckoo is an attractive bird with an unpleasant habit – it doesn't make a nest for its own egg, but lays it in the nest of another bird (usually the grey warbler), and when the cuckoo chick hatches, its first instinct is to push any other chicks or eggs out of the nest.

The grey warbler then raises the cuckoo chick as though it was its own.

The shining cuckoo does not spend winter in New Zealand. Instead, it flies to islands around Papua New Guinea and Indonesia and then returns around September and October.

The bellbird is named for its pretty song, made up of 2–6 clear, bell-like notes. Its song is particularly attractive when several birds are singing together in the early morning.

Like the tui, the bellbird has a brush-like tongue, which helps it to take nectar from native and introduced plants. Males will chase off females from the nectar plants, so the female's diet is mostly insects and spiders.

Weight: 26–34 g	
Length: 20 cm	
Lifespan: 8 years	
Diet: Insects, spiders, fruits and nectar	
Distribution: Common in forested areas, but rare north of Auckland and in much of Canterbury and Otago.	

New Zealand Robin

Weight: 35 g	
Length: 18 cm	
Lifespan: 16 years	
Diet: Insects, spiders, worms and fruits	
Distribution: Central North Island forests, the West Coast and Marlborough regions, though rare	

This forest-dwelling robin likes to perch on low branches, and then swoop down to catch insects such as weta and beetles. Sometimes it will stand on one leg and tremble the other among the leaf litter to encourage hidden insects to move. Like the fantail, the robin will follow walkers on bush tracks and snatch up any disturbed prey – the robin will even fly down onto people's heads or shoulders for a better view!

Weight: 30–40 g	
Length: 18 cm	
Lifespan: 7 years	
Diet: Insects, fruits and nectar	
Distribution: Rare, and only on protected island sanctuaries	

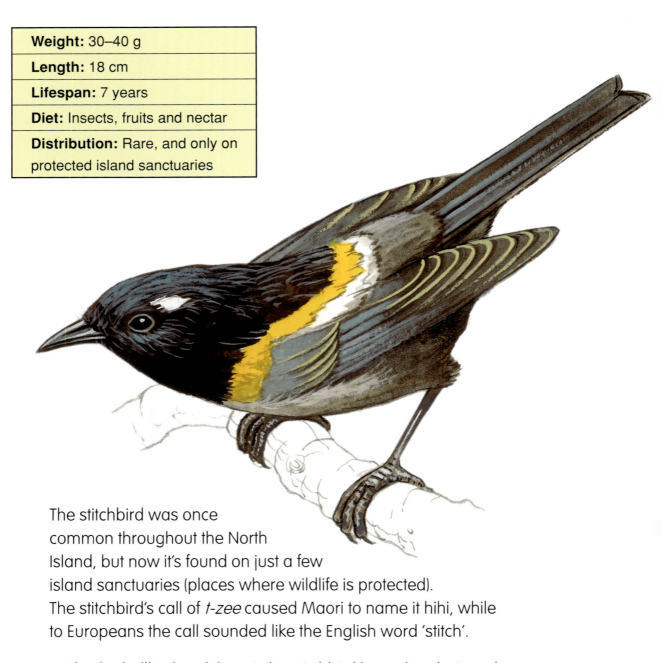

The stitchbird was once common throughout the North Island, but now it's found on just a few island sanctuaries (places where wildlife is protected). The stitchbird's call of *t-zee* caused Maori to name it hihi, while to Europeans the call sounded like the English word 'stitch'.

Like the bellbird and the tui, the stitchbird has a brush-tipped tongue, which enables it to enjoy the nectar of flax, pohutukawa, rata and puriri flowers as well as many other plants.

The male bird, pictured here, is strongly coloured, but the female is much duller, though with the same white 'shoulder'.

Weight: 40–50 g	
Length: 23–25 cm	
Lifespan: 5–7 years	
Diet: Insects, leaves, seeds and fruits	
Distribution: Areas of the West Coast, and forests of the central North Island down to Wellington	

The Maori name for this bird – kakariki – means 'small parrot' and also 'green'.

Once numerous enough to be seen in flocks of tens of thousands, parakeet numbers have been dramatically reduced by hunting and introduced predators, and now it can only be seen in a few forest areas.

Some parakeets will chew the leaves of manuka and kanuka, which contain a natural insecticide (a chemical that kills insects), to spread this through their feathers to control lice.

Saddleback

Weight: 70–80 g	
Length: 25 cm	
Lifespan: 17 years	
Diet: Insects, fruits and nectar	
Distribution: Only on protected offshore islands	

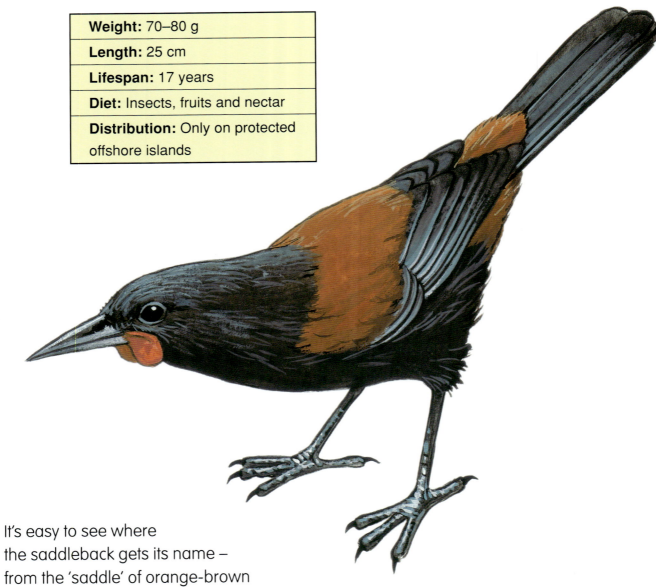

It's easy to see where the saddleback gets its name – from the 'saddle' of orange-brown feathers across its back!

Numbers of saddlebacks have fallen dramatically since the arrival of cats, dogs, rats and weasels. Saddlebacks like to forage for food on the forest floor – noisily rummaging in the leaf litter, and digging at rotten logs with their tough bills, which makes them easy prey for these introduced predators.

Fantails and other small birds will sometimes follow a feeding saddleback, eager to pick up any insects that it might stir up.

Tui

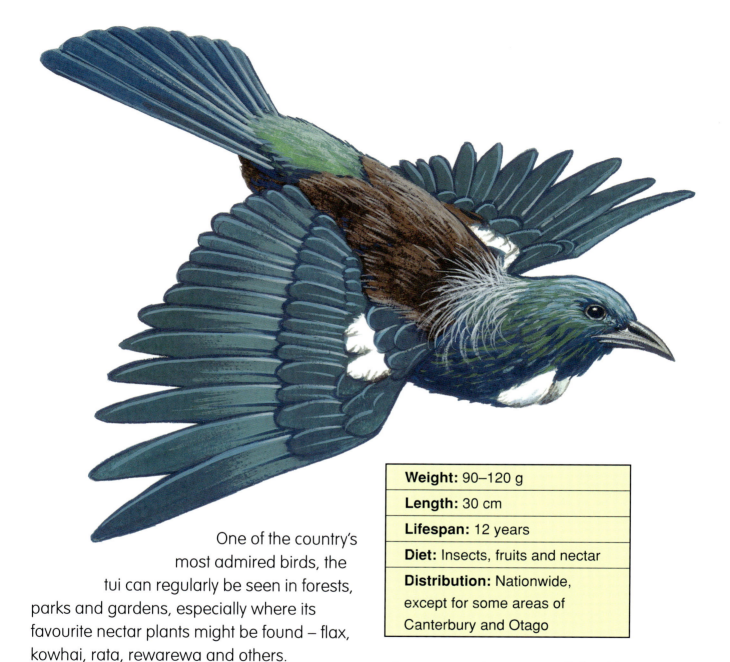

Weight:	90–120 g
Length:	30 cm
Lifespan:	12 years
Diet:	Insects, fruits and nectar
Distribution:	Nationwide, except for some areas of Canterbury and Otago

One of the country's most admired birds, the tui can regularly be seen in forests, parks and gardens, especially where its favourite nectar plants might be found – flax, kowhai, rata, rewarewa and others.

The tui is one of our most talented song birds – often the first to start singing in the morning, and the last to finish in the evening. Sometimes it will even sing into the moonlit night. Its song is a series of clear, liquid notes, plus an amazing range of chuckles, coughs, whistles, twangs and beeps. It can imitate nearly any other bird's song, as well as a range of mechanical devices such as car alarms and phones.

Morepork

Maori named this owl ruru for the sound of its main call, and Europeans called it morepork. However, some people think that its call actually sounds more like *quor-quo*.

Like most owls, the morepork prefers to be active at night, hunting for food. The morepork's excellent sight and hearing, plus the soft feathers on the edges of its wings that help it to fly silently, combine to make it an exceptional hunter.

The morepork has been one of the few native birds to do well after the arrival of human settlers because they brought more small prey for it to catch – mice, rats and small birds such as the chaffinch.

Weight: 175 g	
Length: 29 cm	
Lifespan: 6–10 years	
Diet: Rats, mice, lizards, large insects, small birds, moths and flying insects	
Distribution: Nationwide	

Kokako

The kokako is a rather poor flyer and makes its way through the forest by scrambling, flapping and gliding through the trees and branches.

Kokako eat mostly vegetation of some kind, and usually feed parrot-fashion – perched on one foot, while grasping the food with the other foot.

The blue-coloured folds of skin at the side of its bill show that the kokako is a member of a group of birds known as wattlebirds, which includes the saddleback and the extinct huia. Its name comes from the main part of its song – *ko-ka-kooo*.

Weight: 230 g	
Length: 38 cm	
Lifespan: 20 years	
Diet: Foliage, flowers, fruits and insects	
Distribution: Upper North Island forests	

33

Weight: 475–525 g	
Length: 45 cm	
Lifespan: 20 years	
Diet: Insects, grubs, nectar, fruits, leaves and shoots	
Distribution: Mostly western regions of the South Island, Wellington region and the upper half of the North Island	

The kaka is a type of parrot, and is a close relative of the kea. It's a very good climber, and uses its feet and bill to clamber up and down tree trunks and branches, just like a monkey.

The kaka likes to eat various types of wood-boring beetles, such as the kanuka longhorn beetle, and will spend a long time tearing away rotten bark and wood to get at the grubs beneath.

Kaka prefer to live in forest areas, but will sometimes enter gardens and parks during winter to feed on exotic (introduced) plants.

New Zealand Pigeon

Weight:	650 g
Length:	51 cm
Lifespan:	10 years
Diet: Leaves, flowers, seeds and fruits	
Distribution: Nationwide	

The New Zealand pigeon's main Maori name is kereru, but one of its other names is kuku, which is closer in sound to the bird's main call – *coo-coo*.

The New Zealand pigeon likes to eat a wide variety of fruits such as the berries of puriri, miro, tawa, taraire, nikau and many others.

Before becoming a protected bird, the pigeon was highly prized by Maori and was caught in great numbers for food and for its feathers to use in making cloaks.

The New Zealand pigeon has been seen taking 'showers' in the rain, by hanging over to one side from a branch to get its undersides wet, and then swinging over to the other side to complete the job!

This large, flightless bird is famous for its strong homing ability and its inquisitiveness. In an experiment, one bird managed to find its way home from over 300 kilometres away. Campers need to watch out for the weka, as it will get into tents, huts and gear and eat any food that it might discover, or make off with anything it finds bright and interesting – such as items of cutlery, watches, compasses and so forth.

The weka's diet is wide, and these birds

Weight: 700–1000 g	
Length: 53 cm	
Lifespan: 15–18 years	
Diet: Insects, worms, snails, rats, eggs and small birds	
Distribution: North-west and south-west areas of the South Island, East Cape and some offshore islands	

can become a pest near conservation areas by taking the eggs or young chicks of other ground-dwelling birds.

Brown Kiwi

The kiwi is probably the best known of all New Zealand's birds, and the brown kiwi is the most common of the several kiwi species found in New Zealand. The populations of all species of kiwi have been reduced from many millions down to some tens of thousands, due to them falling prey to dogs, stoats, rats and other introduced animals. They have also suffered from forest clearances and hunting.

Kiwi nest in burrows and emerge at night to forage for food in the forest leaf litter, probing the ground with their long bills to find and dig out earthworms.

The kiwi is flightless, but it does have wings – though they are very small and are hidden under their rough feathers. The little clawed wing makes a good spot for the kiwi to tuck in its bill when it curls up to sleep in its burrow.

Weight: 2200–2800 g	
Length: 400–500 cm	
Lifespan: 20–30 years	
Diet: Insects, grubs, worms, spiders and fallen fruits	
Distribution: Forests of the upper North Island	

Kakapo

Before the arrival of humans, dogs and cats, the flightless kakapo was widespread throughout all of the country, but now their population is less than 100 birds.

The kakapo is the heaviest parrot in the world, and is mostly solitary in its habits. However, when it comes time for the male to find a mate he joins other males to construct bowl-shaped scoops in the ground from where they make booming noises through the night to announce their presence. These deep 'booms' can be heard by females over 7 kilometres away.

Weight: 2000–2500 g	
Length: 63 cm	
Lifespan: 30–40 years	
Diet: Seeds, roots, foliage and shoots	
Distribution: Only in protected sanctuaries on offshore islands	

Takahe

The flightless takahe was once widespread throughout New Zealand. It was actually thought to be long extinct until a small population was discovered in a remote valley in the South Island in 1948.

The takahe looks like a much larger version of the pukeko, and it's thought that both birds share the same distant ancestor.

Takahe are very territorial, and some males will even rush to attack human intruders during the breeding season.

Young takahe sometimes stay with their parents for up to 18 months, and may help to raise younger chicks.

Weight: 3000 g	
Length: 63 cm	
Lifespan: 14–20 years	
Diet: Tussock stems and shoots, seeds and fern roots	
Distribution: Rare – only on protected island sanctuaries and a small population in the South Island.	

39

Weight: 350 g	
Length: 38 cm	
Lifespan: 12–16 years	
Diet: Grubs, caterpillars and earthworms	
Distribution: Nationwide, except for Fiordland	

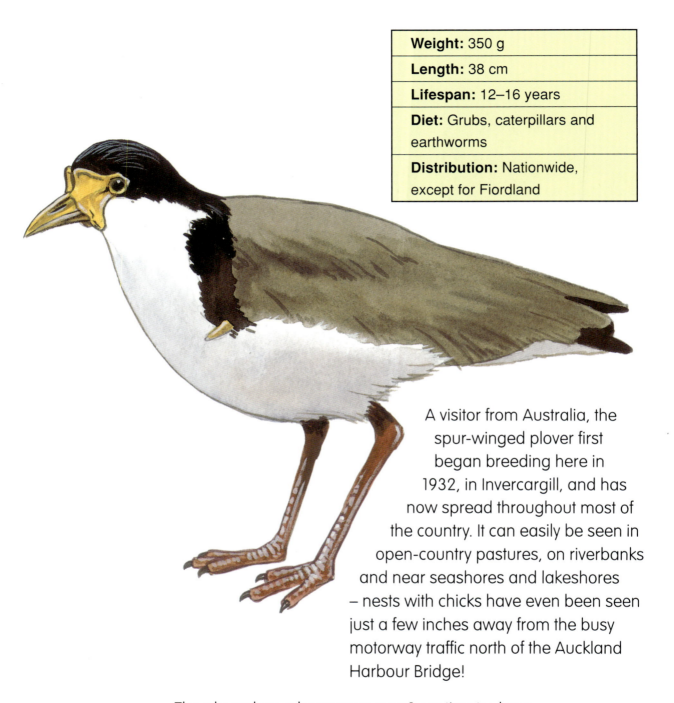

A visitor from Australia, the spur-winged plover first began breeding here in 1932, in Invercargill, and has now spread throughout most of the country. It can easily be seen in open-country pastures, on riverbanks and near seashores and lakeshores – nests with chicks have even been seen just a few inches away from the busy motorway traffic north of the Auckland Harbour Bridge!

The plover has a bony spur over 1 centimetre long on the front of its wing, which it can use as a weapon to defend its nest against predators such as the Australasian harrier and the Australian magpie.

Little Owl

The little owl – also known as the German owl or the brown owl – was introduced into the South Island from Germany in 1906, when finches and sparrows were becoming too much of a problem on Otago farms. However, it was soon found that the little owl much preferred to eat insects and spiders!

Unlike most other owls, the little owl hunts mostly in the daytime, and can often be seen perched on posts, power poles and hedges as it keeps a lookout for prey. It will also walk and run around on the ground as it looks for food.

If disturbed, the little owl performs a comical display of bobbing up and down, and rotating its head to help judge the nearness of the intruder.

Weight: 180 g	
Length: 23 cm	
Lifespan: 10 years	
Diet: Insects, spiders, earthworms and small animals	
Distribution: Mostly the east coast of the South Island, especially the Otago region	

Weight: 500 g	
Length: 47 cm	
Lifespan: 6–10 years	
Diet: Large insects, rodents, lizards and small birds	
Distribution: Central North Island and most of the South Island, except for areas of Southland and Canterbury	

Though it's only half the size of the Australasian harrier, the New Zealand falcon is a much more aggressive bird and will even attack the harrier and other birds in flight, including the tui, the New Zealand pigeon and the Australian magpie. Some falcons will regularly check other birds' nests to prey on newborn chicks.

Mostly, the falcon hunts by watching the countryside from a high perch, and then launching into flight when prey is spotted. It can reach speeds of up to 180 kilometres an hour in a dive. It strikes with its claws and then makes the final kill with a bite from its powerful bill.

Once seen as a threat to farm birds, the falcon was regularly shot until it became a protected bird in 1970.

Kea

Weight: 1000 g	
Length: 46 cm	
Lifespan: 15–20 years	
Diet: Fruits, seeds, insects and carrion (dead animals)	
Distribution: High country of the South Island only; mostly western regions	

Named for its call of *kee-aa*, this cheeky parrot has been reckoned by some to be one of the most intelligent of all birds, with its strongly inquisitive nature and ability to solve complex puzzles.

Visitors to the Southern Alps can be both charmed and annoyed by the kea's behaviour; it likes to 'ski' down the corrugated iron roofs of huts, and to investigate any unattended campers' or trampers' equipment, taking off with anything remotely interesting or edible – even stripping the seals from car windscreens or ripping sleeping bags apart.

Many tens of thousands of kea were killed by early settlers, as they were seen as a danger to sheep, but they have been protected since 1986.

43

Australasian Harrier

Weight: 850 g	
Length: 60 cm	
Lifespan: 18 years	
Diet: Rabbits, hares, rats, lizards, small birds, large insects, frogs and carrion (dead animals). Some harriers will even go 'fishing' for fish and tadpoles.	
Distribution: Nationwide	

You'll usually see this big bird of prey circling above farmland and scrub as it searches the ground for small animals, or in the middle of the road feeding on the carcasses of hedgehogs and possums that have been struck by cars.

When much of New Zealand was covered in forest, many centuries ago, there were not many harriers here, but their numbers have increased dramatically as much of the country has become open land, and with the arrival of small animals, such as rats and rabbits, for them to feed on.

44

Pied Stilt

Weight: 190 g	
Length: 35 cm	
Lifespan: 12 years	
Diet: Shellfish, insects and worms	
Distribution: Nationwide, except for Fiordland	

The pied stilt is a relatively recent arrival from Australia – it probably arrived during the early 1800s. They can be seen around estuaries, mudflats, wetlands and pasturelands throughout most of the country, wading through the water on their stilt-like legs and probing the soft mud or sand with their long bills to seek out their food. When inland, these birds will feed on water-insects and worms, and when at the coast they will look for shellfish.

While the numbers of pied stilt have increased over the years as forests have been replaced by farms and open country, its close relative the black stilt has declined dramatically and is now one of New Zealand's rarest birds.

Red-Billed Gull

Weight:	260–300 g
Length:	37 cm
Lifespan:	28 years
Diet:	Shellfish, fish, insects, worms and carrion (dead animals)
Distribution:	Most New Zealand coasts

This smallish gull is very easy to spot around the coasts, with its red bill and its distinctive noisy call of *scrark*. Like its much larger cousin, the black-backed gull, this bird will scavenge for food scraps in all sorts of unusual places – parks, rubbish dumps, supermarket car parks and so on.

The young red-billed gull actually has a black bill, and can be confused with the black-billed gull, which usually lives further inland. And just to confuse things further, the young black-billed gull has a pinkish-red bill, similar to the red-billed gull …!

Blue Penguin

This is the world's smallest penguin and the most common of all the penguin species found around New Zealand. The blue penguin is also known as the little blue penguin or the fairy penguin and can be seen singly or in small groups in harbours and inner coastal waters.

Although it spends most of its time at sea, the blue penguin returns to land to roost and nest in caves, vegetation, burrows or even under houses and outbuildings. Some birds will walk inland for up to a kilometre to find a suitable spot.

Weight: 1100 g	
Length: 40 cm	
Lifespan: 19 years	
Diet: Small fish and squid	
Distribution: Various coastal regions, especially the upper North Island and the lower South Island	

47

Pied Oystercatcher

Weight: 550 g	
Length: 46 cm	
Lifespan: 20–27 years	
Diet: Shellfish, small fish, insects and worms	
Distribution: Throughout the South Island during summer, and around North Island coasts in winter	

This distinctive bird can be seen in small or large flocks (sometimes numbering many thousands of birds) near the coasts around most of the country.

The oystercatcher's long, stout bill is used to probe for shellfish in the sand. It then opens the shells by stabbing the bill between the two halves and twisting them open to get at the animal inside. Some oystercatchers are even strong enough to stab right through the shell.

The variable oystercatcher is a close relative, though slightly larger, and has less obvious 'shoulder straps'. Sometimes all-black birds can be seen.

48

Black-Backed Gull

This bird is by far the largest and the most distinctive of New Zealand's gulls, with its black back and wings making it very easy to spot.

The black-backed gull is a great scavenger, and seems capable of eating just about anything even remotely edible. It will look for food in all sorts of places – estuaries, shorelines (sometimes following boats far out to sea), rubbish dumps, farms (some gulls will take dead or weak lambs), sewer outlets, rubbish dumps and so on. Besides seeing these gulls at all these places, have a look at your local street lamps – chances are that the large bird perched on top is a black-backed gull!

Weight: 800–1000 g	
Length: 60 cm	
Lifespan: 28 years	
Diet: Shellfish, worms, insects and carrion (dead animals)	
Distribution: Nationwide	

The young black-backed gull is called ngoiro, and because of its appearance is sometimes thought to be a different species of bird. This 'teenager' can seem awkward and clumsy – when pigeons, sparrows and gulls gather around picnickers for handouts, poor ngoiro can usually be seen at the back of the bunch, wondering how to get some of the goodies on offer!

49

Weight: 2000 g	
Length: 81 cm	
Lifespan: 20 years	
Diet: Fish, shrimp and crayfish	
Distribution: Most coasts, except the Wanganui region	

One of the most common of the 12 species of shag in New Zealand, the pied shag makes its nest in trees around estuaries, shorelines and lakes. Sometimes the trees suffer a great deal from the shags' heavy landings, their sprawling nests and even from the large amounts of shag droppings.

Shags dive into the water to catch mullet, eels, flounder and other fish, and can stay underwater for around 30 seconds. Afterwards they will perch with their wings outspread to dry out, as their feathers lack any waterproof oils.

50

Yellow-Eyed Penguin

Known to Maori as hoiho, this is probably the world's rarest penguin, with a population of only about 5000, and it's found only around New Zealand.

Just like the blue penguin, the yellow-eyed penguin likes to come ashore regularly to roost and nest in vegetation and hollows in the ground, often quite some distance from the coast.

The yellow-eyed penguin is a very good swimmer, and can dive to depths of over 160 metres (twice the depth of a typical blue penguin dive) to catch bottom-dwelling fish and squid.

Weight: 5400 g	
Length: 65 cm	
Lifespan: 30 years	
Diet: Fish and squid	
Distribution: Banks Peninsula, and Otago and Southland coasts	

Weight:	400 g
Length:	66 cm
Lifespan:	14 years
Diet:	Fish, shellfish and crabs
Distribution:	Mostly around rocky coasts, except for the West Coast and some areas north of Wellington

The reef heron can be seen along shorelines as it carefully stalks the water's edge to seek out prey. It often holds up one wing as it walks, to shade the water and to cut out reflections.

Because it always feeds near the water's edge at low tide, it can be seen out foraging at different times of the day – or even at night. Some reef herons will enter colonies of other birds, such as terns, and steal food intended for chicks.

The general Maori name for herons is matuku, and the reef heron is known as matuku tai or matuku moana.

White-Faced Heron

The white-faced heron became established here from Australia in the 1940s. It has now spread throughout the country – around all kinds of coasts, in farmlands and pastures, wetlands, estuaries and even sewage treatment ponds. It's now the most common of all the herons in New Zealand.

The white-faced heron often finds food by standing in shallow water and raking the ground to stir up any small fish or other prey.

The Maori name for this heron is matuku moana.

Weight: 550 g	
Length: 67 cm	
Lifespan: 8–12 years	
Diet: Fish, frogs, worms, mice and insects	
Distribution: Nationwide	

Australasian Gannet

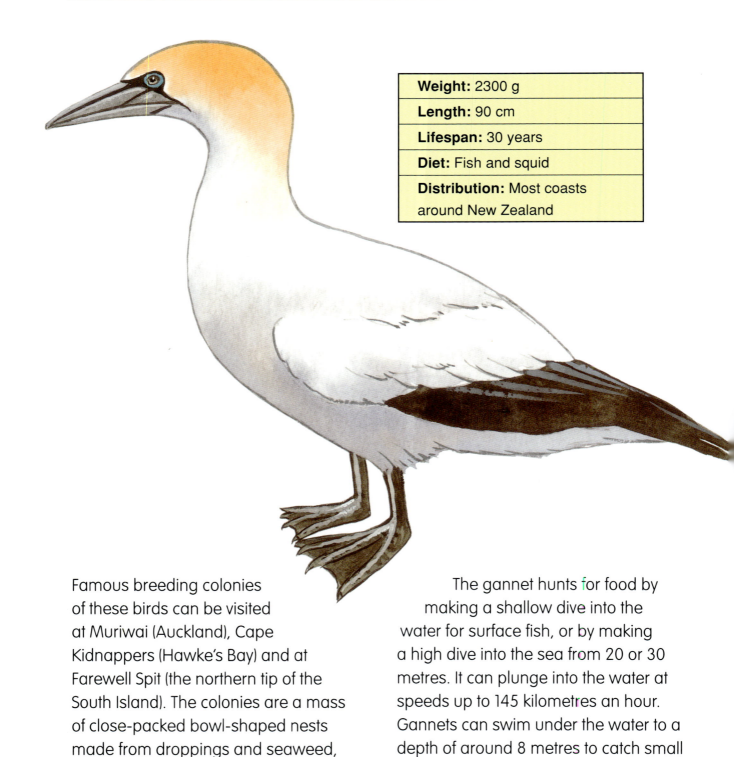

Weight: 2300 g	
Length: 90 cm	
Lifespan: 30 years	
Diet: Fish and squid	
Distribution: Most coasts around New Zealand	

Famous breeding colonies of these birds can be visited at Muriwai (Auckland), Cape Kidnappers (Hawke's Bay) and at Farewell Spit (the northern tip of the South Island). The colonies are a mass of close-packed bowl-shaped nests made from droppings and seaweed, and populated by squabbling, fighting, arguing, noisy birds!

The gannet hunts for food by making a shallow dive into the water for surface fish, or by making a high dive into the sea from 20 or 30 metres. It can plunge into the water at speeds up to 145 kilometres an hour. Gannets can swim under the water to a depth of around 8 metres to catch small fish such as anchovies, mullet, pilchards and small squid.

White Heron

This heron likes to hunt for food in swamps, wetlands and estuaries, where it will stand motionless or walk very carefully and quietly until it sees its prey and lunges at it with its large bill. It is so fast in its strike that it can even take small birds such as the silvereye and the kingfisher.

The white heron is by far the largest of all the heron species in New Zealand, and is known to Maori as kotuku.

Weight: 900 g	
Length: 82 cm	
Lifespan: 22 years	
Diet: Fish, frogs, mice, small birds and insects	
Distribution: Various coasts around the country, but especially those of the West Coast, and north of the Waikato	

The white heron can be seen near coasts around much of the country, though it's quite a rare bird, with less than 200 individuals.

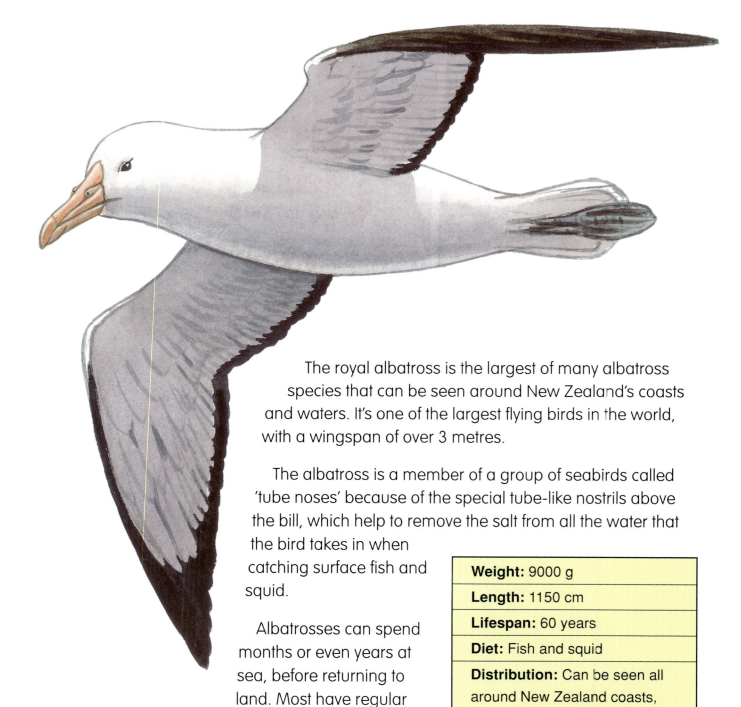

The royal albatross is the largest of many albatross species that can be seen around New Zealand's coasts and waters. It's one of the largest flying birds in the world, with a wingspan of over 3 metres.

The albatross is a member of a group of seabirds called 'tube noses' because of the special tube-like nostrils above the bill, which help to remove the salt from all the water that the bird takes in when catching surface fish and squid.

Albatrosses can spend months or even years at sea, before returning to land. Most have regular circuits that they follow around the southern oceans, as they glide and soar in their search for food.

Weight: 9000 g	
Length: 1150 cm	
Lifespan: 60 years	
Diet: Fish and squid	
Distribution: Can be seen all around New Zealand coasts, but Taiaroa Head on the Otago Peninsula is the royal albatross's only mainland breeding site.	

56

Welcome Swallow

The welcome swallow first arrived in Northland, New Zealand from Australia during the 1950s, and has now spread through most of the country. They can be seen swooping and darting in open country, or over water, as they catch flying insects such as flies, moths and small beetles.

The swallow makes a bowl-shaped nest from a mixture of mud and grass, and it's usually built in protected places like the undersides of bridges or under the overhangs and ledges of houses, sheds and garages.

Weight: 14 g	
Length: 15 cm	
Lifespan: 5–6 years	
Diet: Insects	
Distribution: Nationwide, except for most of the South Island's West Coast	

57

Kingfisher

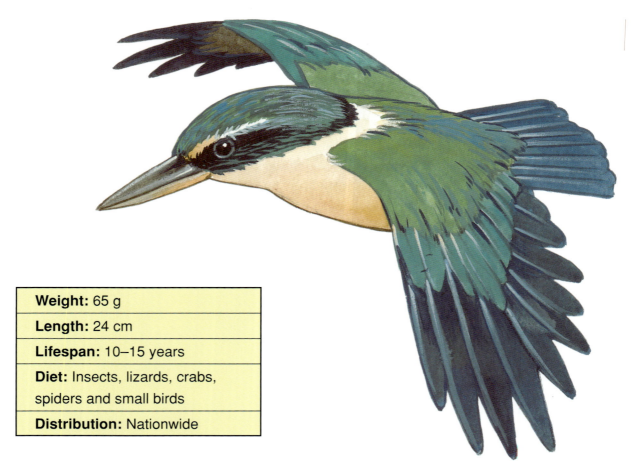

Weight: 65 g	
Length: 24 cm	
Lifespan: 10–15 years	
Diet: Insects, lizards, crabs, spiders and small birds	
Distribution: Nationwide	

Though the kingfisher can be found throughout the country, it's more common in the North Island, and usually moves closer to the coast in the winter. It can be seen on perches near water, such as telephone and power lines, where it keeps a watch for any movement from likely prey such as lizards, insects or crabs on mudflats. Sometimes it will prey on mice or even on small birds like the silvereye. The kingfisher will even rob other birds of the earthworms they've caught.

The kingfisher usually makes a nest in earth banks and cuttings. It starts the tunnels by flying directly at the bank and striking with its heavy bill. Once the hole is deep enough, the kingfisher will perch and start digging; it works away until the tunnel is about 10–20 centimetres long, and with a wide chamber at the end.

Blue Duck

Weight: 750–900 g	
Length: 53 cm	
Lifespan: 13 years	
Diet: Water insects	
Distribution: The mountain rivers of central and western regions of the South Island and the central North Island	

The blue duck likes to live in and around fast-flowing mountain rivers, where it feeds on water insects. It catches the insects by scraping them off the river rocks with its bill – the end of the bill is protected by a special tip of soft, black skin.

When the chicks are born, they already have large feet to help them adapt quickly to life in and around the rushing waters of mountain rivers.

The Maori name for this duck is whio, because of its soft, whistling call of *whee-oh*.

Pukeko

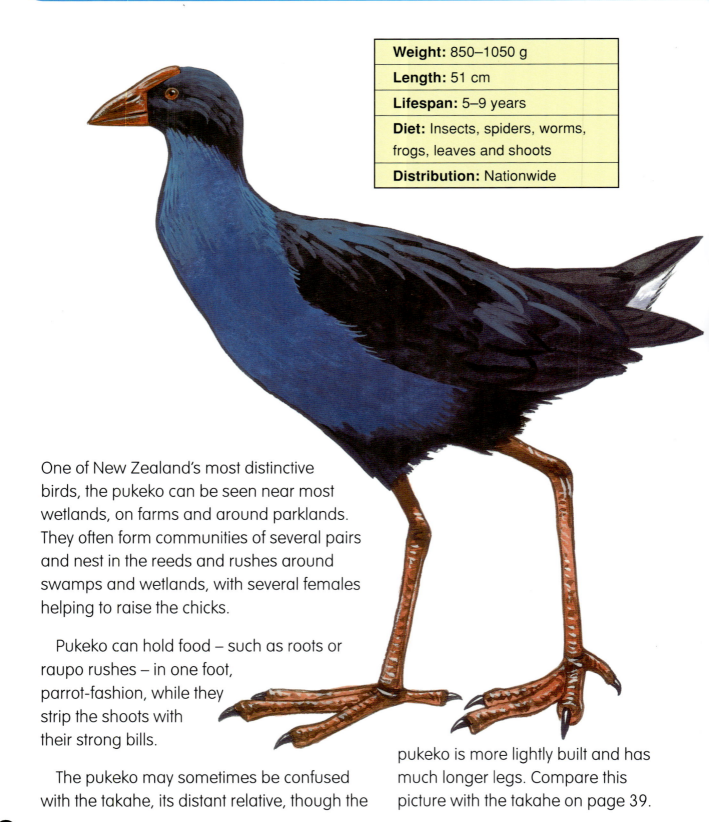

Weight: 850–1050 g	
Length: 51 cm	
Lifespan: 5–9 years	
Diet: Insects, spiders, worms, frogs, leaves and shoots	
Distribution: Nationwide	

One of New Zealand's most distinctive birds, the pukeko can be seen near most wetlands, on farms and around parklands. They often form communities of several pairs and nest in the reeds and rushes around swamps and wetlands, with several females helping to raise the chicks.

Pukeko can hold food – such as roots or raupo rushes – in one foot, parrot-fashion, while they strip the shoots with their strong bills.

The pukeko may sometimes be confused with the takahe, its distant relative, though the pukeko is more lightly built and has much longer legs. Compare this picture with the takahe on page 39.

Grey Duck

The grey duck used to be the most common duck in New Zealand, but since the arrival of the mallard its numbers have reduced dramatically because the mallard has taken over much of the grey duck's usual habitats. Nowadays, the grey duck is mostly seen around the lakes and rivers of more remote regions.

The grey duck is very similar in appearance to the female mallard, but has a green panel of feathers (a speculum) on its wing where the mallard has a blue-purple panel.

Although some birds can live for 20 years or more, most have a life expectancy of just 2 or 3 years.

Weight: 1000–1100 g	
Length: 55 cm	
Lifespan: 20 years	
Diet: Insects, snails, worms, seeds and plant material	
Distribution: Nationwide	

Mallard

The mallard was first introduced into New Zealand in 1867 and has now become the most common and the most easily seen duck. It's very common in parks, estuaries, rivers and farms and often becomes familiar with humans and tame enough to be fed by hand. In places where they are used to getting hand-outs, they'll follow visitors in a quacking bunch, pecking at ankles until they get fed.

Some mallards can live up to 26 years or so but, like the grey duck, most only live for a couple of years.

Weight: 1100–1300 g	
Length: 58 cm	
Lifespan: 26 years	
Diet: Insects, freshwater snails, seeds and water plants	
Distribution: Nationwide	

Australasian Bittern

The bittern is a bird that's usually heard rather than seen. It lives deep in the close reeds and rushes of swamps and wetlands, and the male bird announces his presence and his territory by making a deep booming noise (you can make the same noise by blowing across the top of a bottle).

Bitterns are solitary birds, and if a male stumbles into another's territory, they will fight and stab each other with their strong bills.

Weight: 1000–1400 g	
Length: 71 cm	
Lifespan: 10–15 years	
Diet: Insects, rats, mice, eels and frogs	
Distribution: Nationwide, though rare	

If disturbed, the bittern will 'freeze' with its bill pointed skywards, to try and blend in with the surrounding reeds. Its eyes are so placed that it can still see all around in this position. If it's a windy day, the bittern will even sway slightly along with the reeds.

Index

(**Bold** numbers refer to main entries)